My Year Off Men

My Year
Off
Men

What Happened When I Took a Year Off
the Search for a Man to Search Within

Kelly Alexander B.A. B.Ed.

BALBOA.
PRESS
A DIVISION OF HAY HOUSE

Balboa Press books may be ordered through booksellers or by contacting:

Balboa Press
A Division of Hay House
1663 Liberty Drive
Bloomington, IN 47403
www.balboapress.com
1 (877) 407-4847

Because of the dynamic nature of the Internet, any web addresses or links contained in this book may have changed since publication and may no longer be valid. The views expressed in this work are solely those of the author and do not necessarily reflect the views of the publisher, and the publisher hereby disclaims any responsibility for them.

The author of this book does not dispense medical advice or prescribe the use of any technique as a form of treatment for physical, emotional, or medical problems without the advice of a physician, either directly or indirectly. The intent of the author is only to offer information of a general nature to help you in your quest for emotional and spiritual well-being. In the event you use any of the information in this book for yourself, which is your constitutional right, the author and the publisher assume no responsibility for your actions.

Disclaimer: The names of most people have been changed to protect their privacy unless permission was given to use real names. The locations in the book have been slightly altered as well but in no way compromise the integrity of the story.

Author Photo: Suvi Naga: Sin-Design & Photography
Edited by Amy Scott of Nomad Editorial

Printed in the United States of America.

ISBN: 978-1-4525-8755-4 (sc)
ISBN: 978-1-4525-8756-1 (e)

Balboa Press rev. date: 12/04/2013

"I'm happily, more serenely and healthily pursuing my divine purpose on earth thanks to Kelly's spiritually nourishing support."

~ Mariam Fazlollahi, Reiki Master ~

Praise for Kelly Alexander

"Kelly Alexander's book, *My Year Off Men,* speaks to women of any age seeking to discover who they really are. Kelly's "Notes to Self" and "Reflections" at the end of each chapter are insightful signposts for the reader on her path to self discovery."

Antoinette Asimus, Coach, Facilitator and Senior Teaching Faculty, Tantra Heart, LLC.

————

"Thank Goddess for Kelly who shows soul sisters of the earth through her own captivating story, the formula for a successful relationship: self love, green smoothies, dancing in Dubai, and one transformational, soul-searching year without men. A fun and inspirational book for single women everywhere!"

Patricia Tomasi, Author of Kick Ass Dreams

————

"MYOM" was a truly honest look at the pitfalls that women fall into to be in a relationship. I recommend this book for the person who has been searching for love outside of themselves."

Helen Everest, Author of Finding Home: the Journey Within

————

"Kelly's love, light, wisdom, beautiful and fun energy has inspired me and changed my life in so many ways. I'm grateful that the Universe made our paths cross at a time when I needed her help most. I experienced the wonders of feeding my body with living – and YUMMY! – food, and my soul with loving, positive thoughts. I have a new appreciation of myself and others . I'm happily, more serenely and healthily pursuing my divine purpose on earth thanks to Kelly's spiritually nourishing support."

Mariam Fazlollahi, Reiki Master

"Kelly has the ability to bring out the best in people with her positive energy, ability to empower, uplift and support others. Kelly is a talented and creative soul and a healthy and vibrant woman. She carries authentic communication and lovely leadership!"

Christine Anonuevo, Community Economic Developer

"Kelly is someone you just love to be around. Every moment with Kelly is a new adventure with lots of laughs leaving a great memory to always look back on and smile! Kelly is someone you can talk to easily without ever feeling embarrassed about whatever the situation may be. Kelly understands that life is all about learning and she is a great leader/coach/listener/friend to help you along your journey."

Miranda Haasnoot, Make-up Artist

"After concluding my first session I am feeling not only relaxed but ready to take on anything that comes my way. Keep up what you are doing, it's such a fulfillment."

Anonymous

"I realized I have never allowed myself true pleasure. I thank you for that in opening me up more."

Anonymous

"I released an issue from my childhood that shaped my sexual identity. I have indeed changed my perception about my sexuality in a great, big, wonderful way. Thank you."

Anonymous

"I recommend Kelly to assist you to find that inner source of delight. I look forward to practicing and expressing."

Anonymous

"Kelly has an aura of joy and enthusiasm that is contagious. This is naturally instinctive to her and her commitment to reaching goals is inspirational. There is no doubt life coaching is her natural place in this universe - she is someone you definitely want on your team."

Anonymous

"Kelly is a beautiful as they come. I am inspired by her every day."

Anonymous

"Kelly is a loving individual with a beautiful glowing energy. One on one she meets me where I'm at, listens objectively and offers enlightened, empowering guidance. Kelly is an incredible role model for women and children leading by example teaching us to love and care for ourselves, each other, and our mother earth."

Anonymous

"Kelly is an inspiring and remarkable human being who manifests great things in her own and other people's lives. I wish I lived in a closer part of the world to her."

Anonymous

"Kelly is one of the most inspiring women I've known. She has traveled around the world and experienced so many different things and interacted with so many different cultures and personalities. She is always willing to try something new and she gives everything and everyone the chance they deserve. Kelly has the utmost positive outlook on life and she is always smiling. She is always there to listen when someone needs to talk, she is very trustworthy and she has that special something about her that can always lift someone's spirit no matter how low they might feel. Kelly's a kind-hearted soul and her energetic spirit is contagious and I feel like it brings out the best in everyone she comes in contact with. When it comes to Kelly, I could go on and on about how great she is, the truth is you will never meet anyone like Kelly, she is truly one of a kind!"

Anonymous

———————

"Kelly is AMAZING! She always sees the glass as half full. She is adventurous, she is a natural leader. She inspires me with every encouraging word she utters! I am blessed to have Kelly as a dear and close friend! Kelly brings love and light to all that know her! Love ya sista!"

Anonymous

———————

*To all my Soul Sisters out there
who deserve a "man-batical."*

Contents

Part III

Acknowledgments

I would like to give enormous gratitude to the universe for blessing me with a life of abundance, supportive parents and the most wonderful brother, whom I'm thankful for every day.

I wish to express my deep fondness for my soul sisters on Vancouver Island and in Mainland Canada, Mexico, and the UAE. You know who you are, and you all amaze me with your resilience in the face of certain dating deterrents.

I would like to honor the many men in my life, sweet and sour, who have unwittingly taught me many of the lessons in this book; it would not have been written without you.

I want to express my heartfelt thanks to my wonderful editor, Amy Scott of Nomad Editorial, without whom I would not have been able to pull this off.

Finally, I would like to thank my maker, whoever she is, for always giving me everything I need, even when I don't think I need it.

~ So Much Love ~

Introduction

Tell me if this sounds familiar. I've done it time and time again, and maybe you have too: I have awesome girlfriends, get a boyfriend, lose touch with girlfriends, and lose myself. Then, when the relationship ends, I can't remember what I used to love to do, because I have adopted the things *he* loved to do. I feel so lost and hopeless because I'm alone again, with no idea how to make myself happy. Worse, I have fewer friends and I can't remember why I was so great in the first place.

I didn't want to keep repeating this pattern, so I decided it was time to make some changes. First, I started to notice the clues. I learned that a good way to know if I'm losing myself as the center of my world is if I have *never* liked football, hunting, skeet shooting, or watching hockey, but am doing all these things. If this is occurring in my life, chances are high I have melted into my man and am starting the disappearing process, again. When I see myself being knocked off my center, I can stop the process by asking myself, *What do I love to do? What is important to me? And who am I on my own?* If I answer these questions and stay true to me, from here on out I will be aware of when I am slipping into the man abyss.

My Year off Men (MYOM) showed me the answers to these very personal questions. I had just suffered another heartbreak at the hands of a man I envisioned growing old with, and I decided I needed to take some time away from men and relationships to focus on myself. Thanks to MYOM, I see that in many of my relationships we had nothing in common but each other, and that I totally became who he wanted me to be and not who I needed to become for myself. Now, when I get involved with another man, I am able to recognize when I start to drop out of orbit to circle around *his world* instead of my own. When I see this now, I can quickly reestablish my own personal gravity and get back to my center.

You might be under the impression that this book is a man-hating guide to giving up. But even if it kind of did start out that way, it actually turned out to be the exact opposite. I love men. Good men. And after taking my *man-batical* to establish some healthy personal boundaries, I am able to see clearly now in regards to what I want in a partnership. These personal boundaries guide me now, as opposed to when I would date a man just because he was into me without finding out if we had anything in common (which, surprisingly enough, turns out to be the foundation for a relationship).

This is a book about me and my journey, but maybe about you and your journey too. It's my insight into MYOM, which gave me an opportunity to get to know me and what *I* want. MYOM was about loving myself so much that I began to see that I've been enough all along and don't need a man to fulfill me. Always searching outside of myself for that fulfillment left me single and alone in my thirties. If my twenties had taught me anything, it was that in this next decade, my fulfillment was going to have to come from the inside out, not the other way around.

It is my deepest hope that you will see yourself in parts of my journey and that through my story you will learn valuable lessons about your own journey. Perhaps you will see that you have been taking on his dreams and sacrificing your own. Perhaps you will see that you have been setting your standards way lower than you deserve. Or perhaps you will see that you have never taken any time to get to know your beautiful self and that perhaps it's time to take your own year off men to do just that.

The most important things I can share with you from my journey are the lessons I have learned. I hope they help you realize that your YOM, should you choose to take one, will probably not be an all-or-nothing experience, and that's okay. You are going to stumble and fall and revert back to old patterns like I did, but you will be aware of it when it happens and you'll learn what to do about it for your future sanity. Remember, if we lose our center, there are many magical soul sisters out there who can help us get re-centered as well. When I took MYOM, it was my soul sisters who pulled me through, supported me, and cheered me on, and I hope that through this book I'm able to provide the same support for you.

Please go through *My Year off Men* any way you like: read it or use it as a shield to fend off unwanted advances. However you use the book, I highly recommend that you respond to the reflections at the end of each chapter, hopefully in your journal. I've created them based on my own year off men, and I hope that thinking about these experiences will help you get unstuck from those gluey patterns that are stopping you from putting yourself first.

So, my sweet soul sister, I wish you the best of luck, a lot of laughs, some cleansing cries, and, most of all, the space and time a YOM will give you to get to know yourself. If you make the decision to take this next year off men to focus on yourself, I hope the story of my journey provides support and comfort, and I do have some advice: Don't beat yourself up if and when you fall off the proverbial wagon. Be prepared for the universe to test your resolve. Enjoy my Notes to Self (NTS) as silly and sometimes serious asides to my learning journey. Finally, understand that taking a YOM will most likely open you up to a whole new wonderful love: you.

Part I

Chapter 1

Summer
How It All Started

Early one warm summer night, after I had given up my apartment and was couch surfing (again), I was feeling restless. It was only 8 p.m. on a Tuesday and my friend who was hosting me had gone to bed. My job contract had just finished, as well as the vague romance I'd called a relationship, so like I said, I felt restless about what I was going to do now. Evidently, the relationship I'd been in had been in my head, as I was not staying at *his* house and he had only shown up to my farewell party for five minutes. He certainly was not torn apart over my leaving.

Of course, I took that opportunity in the early night hours to creep on him on Facebook (oh, how the time goes by when creeping), but then an ad sparked my interest. I ended up on a recruiter's site that had me dreaming of warm gulf breezes and flying-carpet rides. Figuring it was better than wasting my time on yet another nothing-in-common lover, I applied to the posting and went to bed. In the morning, I had a job offer. Yowza, that happened just about as fast as many of my romances!

Now, going back east for a month to tell your family and friends you have just accepted a two-year contract to work in the Middle East is a feat in itself. Just as when I had moved to Mexico and many people thought my beloved Mexicans were sombrero-wearing, mariachi singers, many felt that all of the Middle East was filled with terror. Without a doubt, nothing was further from the truth, but try telling this to a family who watches the news religiously and can tell you every awful thing that's happening in the world on any given day. It's not their fault, though; it's the culture of fear we live in. It was up to me to overcome the fear-filled voices in my head and go on my Middle Eastern adventure.

Naturally, a month before I left on my adventure I met this super-cute guy who became my very brief boyfriend. He at least drove me to the airport to say goodbye—a shade better than my love out west, who barely seemed to care that I was leaving. Finally arriving in the Middle East, this free-flying bird hit a glass window and was plummeted into a culture so very different from her *Vagina Monologue*–ing, gay pride–supporting, veggie-eating one back home. I'd left my spiritual community behind, and now I was all alone. I felt incredibly homesick, and guess who was not there to pick up my call? Evidently, our airport goodbye was the last time I was going to hear from my latest love.

Within a week of arriving, though, a new fella I met at the hospital (I got such bad food poisoning) told me my "boyfriend" had probably met someone else. Ouch. (But he was probably right.) After a week of trying, I finally got my latest love on the phone. As he told me about an "interesting" woman he had met, my intuition told me his meeting her meant something more to him, and I decided to end it. I mean, who was I kidding? We had only been together a month and I had just left for two years. It was time to set us both free. So, once I was a free agent again, I picked up with the local guy, because isn't that where all great love stories start, while giving your stool sample in at the hospital lab? (I was mortified. He had a sense of humor about it.) **NTS:** If he asks me out on a date while I'm handing in my stool sample, I may be in for a surprise later—watch out!

Reflection: How often do you "creep" on a guy you like on Facebook? Does it leave you feeling satisfied or not? Are there any things you can do for yourself to make you feel satisfied internally instead of externally? I personally like to dance in my room and sing a great song at the top of my lungs.

Chapter 2

August–October
The Man Who Broke the Camel's Back
and Made Me Give Up Men (For a Year)

I didn't know I was a blond-haired, blue-eyed target when I got picked up by Hamad in the hospital. I actually thought *I* was doing the picking up. Because he was wearing his dishdasha (a traditional Arabic robe for men that looks like a long white dress) and a white head scarf tied up with what looked like a black rope, I knew he was from the elite Emirati race that everyone talked about as being so elusive. This clearly made me want to get to know him even more. Hamad was not the least bit elusive, however, and actually—as I later learned when he tried to schmooze one of my girlfriends—had a history of picking up female expats. Unfortunately for me he was also amazingly good-looking, with a gorgeous full smile and spectacular body that I could gauge from his well-fitted robe. His most attractive trait, however, was his charisma, and all those surface qualities combined would blind me to his faults for the next few months.

I can't lie; it started out like a fairytale romance. This was a man who took me home from the hospital when I was so sick I could barely walk. Then he would come by every day to make sure I was eating and get me out of my hotel room just to talk or play cards. It was nice to have a friend. Of course, I now recognize that men rarely pay you that kind of attention without having ulterior motives (ah, I was so naive!).

Anyway, Hamad befriended me when I needed a friend, then wined and dined me when I got well. The truth is, in Canada I'd never had a guy romance me before; they are just so into hanging out and hooking up with "no labels," which is really the guy trying to have his cake and also be able to eat more cake, if you know what I mean. I was so over that kind of man, so of course

I was smitten with Hamad's romance—it was the first time I had really experienced it. **NTS:** I deserve to be treated with the chivalry of the 1950s. I'm worth it. It's not anti-feminist; it's just decent.

Over the next few months, he taught me to drive on the bad-ass streets of Dubai so that I was a pro. He also showed me beautiful places I would have never found on my own, like this secret sea park area where we could sit late at night and feel the gulf breezes on our faces. He even helped me move to my new apartment.

My weeks were filled up with beaches, scenic drives, laughter, and passion. But he was never around for long, because he had to go home on the weekends to take care of his sickly mother and father. Did I mention this was every weekend he had to go home? I noticed it was common among my local workmates for females to go home every weekend, but not so much if you were a grown man.

Despite his weekends away, I fell for him. He was all I had there. He was my friend, my guide, and, in some ways, my family. I wanted more. I wanted to meet his family. I wanted to *be* his family. **NTS:** If my guy says his family must not know about me and that I have to be a secret, take it as a huge flashing neon EXIT sign to get the funk out!

I still didn't see this flashing neon sign, and instead pushed and pushed him to introduce me to his family. I wanted so badly to be welcomed into his exclusive club, but in the end I pushed him so hard that I pushed him away. Of course, any guy who really loves you will jump at the chance to show you off to his family and friends, at least I knew that much, so his hedging at introducing me finally told me something was up.

The last night we spent together was Halloween, when we carved our baby pumpkins and he said he had to take an early weekend. I offered to drive him to the airport, but he said he'd get a taxi. It seemed odd to me that he wouldn't accept a free ride, but he must have been feeling the pressure from both sides because after that night, he stopped answering my calls and texts until I finally received it: The breakup text. Are you kidding me?! What a freakin' coward! Perhaps his family made him do it? (Did I still really believe he was visiting his family?) I couldn't catch my breath I was crying so hard. We'd been seeing each other for a whirlwind three months, and not only did I really care for him, he was still my only friend in Dubai. What had I done to end up in this type of dead-end relationship again? **NTS:** Communication with me must be done primarily via phone or face-to-face. None of this constant-text-message BS. Okay, of course here and there a text is fine, but not when days go by and all I get is a one-sentence text that took ten seconds to type. I want to hear a guy's voice, and he will want to hear mine if he's into me. Look, if his ass can accidentally call me when he sits down, then I know his fingers could too if he really wanted to share some of his precious time. My time is just as precious as his.

Reflection: Does he make time for you so that you can actually hear each other's voices? Look for action here on his part. I believe in my soul there is real energy and bonding in actually hearing each other. It might not be super convenient, but do you really want to be with a man who only wants to be with you because you are convenient? In your YOM, try to be extra conscious of a man's words and actions. For example, if he says he's gonna call you, your phone should definitely be ringing. If all is silent, then he is communicating something else, loud and clear.

Chapter 3

November
Greece

I had ignored all the warning signs, and the breakup blindsided me. I didn't know what to do with myself, and a makeover wasn't gonna cut it. I figured, when in doubt, travel, and make over your soul. Nothing says "I'm me again" like a trip, so I booked a flight to Greece, a land that had always seemed so rich and exotic in culture to me. In sixteen hours, I was on my way there. On the plane, I felt it was time to reflect on what I had been willing to give up for a man who clearly would not give up even one thing for me.

The first thing was that our breakup happened to coincide with local holidays in the UAE, and I was *not* invited to celebrate with Hamad's family. My T-shirt-wearing, bare-arm-waving ways were not of their culture and would have insulted them. I get it, and I accept it. However, *he* never seemed to mind it, which showed me that there was some serious hypocrisy in his words and actions. Yet another good sign he was not a good man for me.

The second thing I thought of in my mid-flight reflection was my passion for equality. Would I have been willing to cover my body (something I believe is my birthright to show *or* not to show) using my own, and not the law's, discretion? Would I have been able to celebrate at the beach with his family while wearing a burkini and not feel resentful of all his brothers wearing beach shorts? Could I give up my art career as a feminist performer and painter? How did I almost throw all of that away for a man who *said* all the right things but *did* none of them? **NTS:** In a true partnership, there is no need to give up anything that I am or dream of becoming. A partner is there to support me and my dreams. That is why he's called a "partner."

When I arrived at my hotel in a colorful district of Athens, I felt a bit stronger and a glimmer of my old self was already shimmering back to life. Athens was vibrant: full of life, side-street vendors selling colorful scarves, and ladies with such confidence and ease that I never wanted to leave. These were my women: Strong, confident, and not *needing* a man for their happiness— real bohemian women!

The *great* thing about being in a new city on a solo adventure is that anything is possible because everything is so new and inspiring (ahem, the Acropolis?!). I also had very little space in my brain to go over and over what happened with Hamad, which was a fabulous bonus and a big reason for the trip, honestly. Instead of worrying about what had happened, I was focused on what was happening around me in every glorious moment. In this beautiful city, it was impossible not to be enchanted at every turn.

Now of course you'll say, well, wouldn't you have liked to share that with someone you love? I get that thought, but I have to say, having traveled through Central America with my boyfriend of years gone, I always wondered and sometimes thought how much more fun that trip would've been on my own. I love meeting people, and traveling alone (at least sometimes) is a great way to do that, while letting unplanned and wonderful adventures unfold on my journey.

Also, it was a good chance to ask myself if my traveling enchantment was shareable, anyway. Throughout my life I have always tried to share my joy and wonder with my partners, and quite honestly, it never seemed to work. I remember one warm summer night when I was gazing enraptured at a willow leaf that had moonlit-sparkled dew resting delicately on top of it. I wanted to share that feeling of wonder with the guy I was with, but he just got frustrated, stormed off, and fumed, "I can appreciate it too, just faster than you." I didn't know there was a time limit on enjoyment, but I just nodded to the willow tree in appreciation and went on my way with a man who had no concept of my delight. Perhaps, though, enchantment is all my own, and willing it on someone else defeats the purpose of having those moments that fill my heart right up. Perhaps I am always on my own even when I am with someone, and maybe that's okay.

After two days in Athens, I was completely captivated with this magnificent country, and set off to take a ferry to the island of Crete. On the ferry I met a super-sweet young lady named Lily whom I ended up traveling with. Lily and I stayed in this amazing hostel in a quaint coastal town filled with markets and old shops. We had breakfast out on the cobbled street and ate olives with the best of them. We also met a local woman who invited us to dinner at her home. All of these people were really incredible when I opened up and held welcoming energy to receive them. Travelers and locals alike were all so warm and so inviting, and Lily felt like a soul sister to me. I was renewed, and it had been hours, if not days, since I had thought of Hamad.

On my last night in Greece, I went to the coolest little art bar in Athens, and of course I met a man who wanted to show me the town and take me to dinner. I thanked him but told him I had already seen the city with my friend. And, I didn't tell him this, but I wasn't ready to start dating again; it had only been a week! I needed time to heal the inflicted and self-inflicted pain of dating yet another unavailable man. Besides, it was time to pack up and go back to Dubai, which I wasn't quite sure I really wanted to do. **NTS:** When a guy asks me out for a date, I can take time to decide. I don't have to pounce at the offer; there will be others and I'm worth waiting for.

Reflection: What precious things about yourself have you given up or lost because of a man? What will you do to get them back?

Chapter 4

December
Back to Reality

I began to flourish again on my trip to Greece as I realized I didn't need Hamad to make my two years in the Middle East magical. When I returned to Dubai, I was refreshed and had a whole new outlook on making friends and enjoying the experience of being away from home. Coincidentally, when I'm flourishing and my energy is radiating, men have an eternal tendency to come back to me, like a moth to a flame (have you noticed this too?). When Hamad came crawling back, I was trying to have none of it. I mean, I had all these questions: Why did he do what he did? Why did he disappear on me like that? Why did he ruin our plans for the holidays after he'd said we would go away together? Of course, what I know now is that it doesn't matter why he did what he did, it just matters that he chose to do it. Case closed.

That said, he kept badgering me to meet with him, so very close to Christmas I broke down and let him pick me up for a drive. Have you ever had a man in your life who you know is no good for you, but when you see him there is so much chemistry between the two of you that your resolve goes to hell? Mine did for a moment too, but then I remembered his breakup text message and I pulled myself right back down on planet *me*. I did not waver in my resolve to hold my passion in check, and by the end of our talk he told me he loved me, but was "confused." **NTS:** "I'm so confused" is guy-speak for "I am caught in so many lies, I am sinking in quicksand." It also very likely means that he's looking for some lovin' and he just wants to see if I will sell myself short again for one more romp.

Hearing that he loved me but was "confused," I hoped that he was finally going to tell his family about me, so I did what I always do: I went to Facebook to creep on him. Seeing him post something like "I miss my love and I'm going to tell my family about her" was not in the cards, though. Instead, I saw that his relationship status had indeed changed—to engaged. But not to me, WTF? I could not catch my breath and my whole new resurrected world took a big hit. The shocking news of my recent lover's engagement and the lies as to where he'd probably been going on the weekends crushed me all over again. I started to crumble like a saltine cracker, and my eating became the junkiest-junk-food vegetarian because I just stopped caring about what I put in my mouth and ate to numb the humiliating pain. Insert stomach gurgle.

Nonetheless, I had pulled myself back up before, and I would do it again. But how was I going to stop repeating this thirteen-year pattern? Now that I was so painfully aware of it, it was time to break the cycle. It was finally time to go and make my happiness on my own and never give him a chance to come back. Thank goodness it was almost Christmas and I could get the heck out of this city where everywhere I looked, I saw him. Seriously—locals all wear the same outfit in the UAE; it felt like continual déjà vu and I needed to press pause.

By the time I got home to Canada for Christmas, I was sick. Not a flu or a cold but something much, much worse. I could hardly walk or sneeze due to the pain in my abdomen; it appeared that my crappy diet was catching up with me. Plus, my PMS spiraled out of control along with my monthly moon pain. I lied to my parents about how I was doing because I never talked to them about my personal life. I was humiliated enough without having to share with them that this man, with whom I had talked about growing old together, had so thoroughly duped me. I mean, Hamad and I had jestingly talked about how at ninety he'd still chase me around the house because I'd still be so cute, and that in twenty years it would be amazing to see our children grown. It had felt nice to create a future with him that involved us growing old and wrinkly. He even said it didn't matter how I look because in fifty years I would be all wrinkly and he'd love me anyway.

So, the night that I had creeped on his Facebook page and saw his status change, I was really hurt to discover that it said that he had been with his now-fiancée for three years! I had been the other woman and didn't even know it. How could I have been so blind? Now that I was in so much emotional as well as physical pain, life seemed pretty dark.

As Christmas passed and my time at the 'rents was running thin (I really do love my independence), I was set to go out in Dubai for New Year's Eve. Snazzy, I know. So even though I wasn't feeling any better, I decided to return to the Middle East to make a bang-up New Year if I could.

Reflection: What is your body telling you right now that you are not listening to? Is it a pain? An urge to dance? A feeling of joy or anxiety? Explore how your body is feeling by spending one minute breathing while focusing your breath on that particular feeling. Remember, there is no need to make it either good or bad. Just let the feeling be and honor it regardless.

Part II

Chapter 5

MYOM: January
My Resolution: Any Time of Year

When I arrived at the airport in Dubai, I was whisked home by taxi. This arrival felt very different than the one I'd had when I first arrived months ago. When I arrived the first time in August, it was a little scary but completely exciting and filled with new colleagues I was about to meet. However, this time I was depressed, alone, and still in physical and emotional pain. How had I gotten it so wrong again? Could I really go out that night and put on a brave face in order to perhaps meet some guy in a bar that I might have a smidgen of things in common with? Why did I need a man to define me, make me worthy, and make me feel like I was enough? Most importantly, why did I feel I needed a man to make me feel sensually connected with my own body?

Exhausted after I unpacked, I laid down on my couch. I couldn't muster the energy to get up, and actually, I didn't even want to. So right then, I made the very conscious decision to not go out at all, in order to celebrate this New Year with myself. I was the person I wanted to get to know better and be with this year anyway. I was going to take a conscious year off of dating—a whole year off men. I mean, why did I keep doing this? It was time to break the cycle! I didn't know exactly how to do that but I believed in myself and what my body was telling me. And that it was telling me to listen!

Unfortunately, since it had taken me so long to tune into what my body was saying to me, my physical pain got worse before it got better. So as my mobility decreased daily and my insides bunched up more, my Middle Eastern doctor put pressure on me to have surgery. The ladies I worked with, however, told me I should go back to Canada and not come back until I was better. My endearing Emirati colleague said I definitely should not have the surgery there because in her opinion, they often removed the wrong parts and her dad's friend was still in a coma from his appendectomy. As if my breakup and being alone in a foreign country wasn't bad enough, now I needed surgery? So only two weeks into the new year in Dubai, it looked like I was heading home again. I'd have to live with my mom or my dad and try to figure this shit out. However, as opposed to staying and possibly getting something removed that I couldn't get back, I figured it was worth a try.

The moment I got off the plane in Canada, I decided I was going for broke and let go of all my bad eating habits. No more Tim Horton's double-double, no more toasted bagels with butter and herb-and-garlic cream cheese. Goodbye, milk chocolate, too. I don't know why I did it in exactly that moment, but my body was telling me I needed a serious cleanse. Not to say that I couldn't have rich, dark, organic chocolate someday in the future, but at that moment my body really needed time to heal physically and, dare I say, emotionally. Somehow, I knew the two were very closely connected.

It was a strange time because I had no idea what I was doing nutritionally, but I was at such a breaking point that my body told me I had to give up all this bad comfort food. Oh my God, I was vegan now, and totally on my own when it came to dealing with my friends and family. **NTS:** When I say I've "gone vegan," be prepared for shock and the inevitable "how do you get your protein" question. And finally, be prepared to hear the staunch affirmations from my friends that they could do it too if they just didn't have to give up dairy (which, they don't seem to realize, is really the whole point of a cleanse).

To say I understood the dismay of my friends and family is an understatement; I had been just like them not that long ago. I even remember listening to this musician talk about a raw vegan diet on the radio years earlier; I was like, "Hells no" and changed the station. But at this point, given my healing options, I was all in, *sans* the cheese. **NTS:** Saying I will never do something is like tempting the universe to test me.

On one particularly gut-wrenching morning, I saw another doctor who had yet another opinion of what was wrong with me; he suggested we scrape out my uterus and see where we go from there. Needless to say, the visit really upset me, and I left shaking angry. Thank goodness my mom caught a woman on TV that morning selling her book called *Crazy Sexy Diet* (I am not kidding about the title). Four hours later, I was hobbling out of Chapters with my new veggie bible.

Quite thankfully, the book was everything I needed and more: plant-based eating with a super-spiritual and silly edge. On top of that, the author, Kris Carr, had gone through a super-alarming health scare that inspired her to overhaul her health too. Thankfully, I didn't have cancer like she did, but I felt like I finally had a friend who understood my health challenges. To say it was an emotional and lonely time is the truth, but it was also cleansing and empowering. Even though I still didn't know what I had or didn't have, my body was telling me to stop focusing all my love and energy on men and start taking loving care of me. The universe was showing me again how this was a perfect time to take a YOM to instead do a very much-needed year on me overhaul.

Day in and day out, I woke up, meditated, and made green juice and green smoothies. Slowly, I began to walk almost upright again instead of totally hunched over. Special thanks goes to my mom, who got me all the organic groceries I needed, because I was homeless, jobless, and verging on hopeless. She would insist I keep pursuing my health and not take no for an answer from any doctor. She was my champion when I couldn't be, and to this day I am still so thankful for that.

After that last doctor's appointment went awry, it was clear to me that what I didn't need were more drugs. I had been on birth control pills for years to control my monthly cramps, but this time, my pain was getting worse. It was clear to me that my abdominal pain was not related to my menstrual cycle, yet that was getting increasingly painful in conjunction with my mysterious pain. Luckily a beautiful friend introduced me to Dr. Christiane Northrup, and her book enriched my life too.

Dr. Northrup's book *Women's Bodies, Women's Wisdom,* which I highly recommend to every woman on the planet, connects all the physical to the deeply personal and, yes, spiritual reasons why we women have the unfortunate predisposition to suffer in our menses. She offered creative outlets for my moon cycle, which inspired me and lessened the pain I was feeling all over my uterus, but it did nothing for the pain in my abdomen. So I still didn't actually know what was wrong, and since I had exhausted the medical avenues where my mom lived, I thought I'd go back to my hometown and try out the doctors there, knowing it would be a real treat having to explain to everyone in this small town why I was back.

Reflection: How do you embrace or deny your monthly moon cycle (menses)? What creative activity can you do to nurture yourself during that time, and turn it into something you look forward to instead of dread? I make vision boards for the coming month of what I want to manifest and am always pleasantly surprised at how it shows up in my life.

Chapter 6

MYOM: February
The Town Where I Grew Up

I arrived in my home town only a bit better than when I had flown home to my mom's house near Detroit a few weeks prior. I decided to see one more doctor and then book my flight back to the Middle East where work and my independence called to me (or so I thought).

I didn't even have a chance to make an appointment with a doctor before I had to go straight to emergency because of the increasing pain. The doctor there was so excited to show me an X-ray of my insides; he was almost gleeful at having identified a possible reason why I was in so much pain. I was not as jazzed as he was, but listened to him explain that usually there is a lot of space in the intestines, but mine were completely plugged up (I am paraphrasing here). He suggested I go see yet another specialist. So at least I wasn't full of shit—or maybe I was—but at least someone finally had a viable explanation of why I was in so much pain.

Evidently, the specialists I had seen for my supposed ovary/uterus problem were not the people I needed, so when I finally saw the gastroenterologist, I was relieved. I knew I had found my answer, but was not happy to hear that it involved a complete cleanse and then a scope. So I asked the doctor what he was going to do if the scope turned out positive. He told me the diet change I had started would be his recommended treatment. So then I had to ask myself, why would I go under general anesthesia for that? Seriously. If the treatment options were the same, why would I traumatize my body by having this procedure? I knew in my heart that there was a better way for my body to heal, so I thanked him for his time, left, and booked my plane ticket back to Dubai.

This new diet and new way of life was so different for me and I wasn't exactly sure what I was doing. I thought I was eating well, but I continued to compact my gut. Picture this: Me sitting on the floor at the airport, waiting for my plane and eating my homemade snack. Then picture me doubling over in pain and lying on the airport floor. Believe me, it actually happened. There might have been moaning and rolling too, but I'm not sure I remember too clearly. Then picture the airline staff running over to see if I was okay, and—the final straw—the ambulance team coming to pick me up from the terminal and rushing me out of the airport on a stretcher. Obviously, I was not going to be able to go back to Dubai at that time. Hopefully I could at least get a refund.

I have to say, the emergency ward at the hospital I was rushed to was not very helpful. They told me everything I already knew and offered no new solutions. I was focused on *wellness* and the cause of my symptoms, and here I was seeking help from a *sickness-*managing system. The doctor that offered me drugs as a way to get me out of her ER had no other way to help me. Phrases like "it's just women's issues" and "it's all in your head" need to be erased from modern medical practice. I clearly needed a new plan of action, so back to my dad's I went with my head hung low.

Reflection: What pressing question do you have for your doctor? I realize that as women we tend to not take care of ourselves as well as we take care of our partners, and the YOM is an opportunity to do that, in all areas of your life. So please, make an appointment today if you have a pressing issue, and don't stop until you feel you've got the attention and answer you deserve. Doctors are not gods, but many of them are wonderful people who will do detective work to help you out. Sometimes you just have to be a little persistent or enlist the help of someone who can be pushy for you. (Thanks, Mom.)

Chapter 7

MYOM: March
Nelda

Wen I got back to my dad's after a hellish night at the hospital and a drive through the world's worst snowstorm, I gave up on my dreams of going back to the Middle East and my independent life. My health and my healing would be my full-time job. At least I hadn't even thought of old-what's-his-name in weeks. This time of healing was about me. I needed to utilize every ounce of energy I had for the present journey and not waste it on the past.

Every morning, my dad kept trying to help me get better by getting me outside in the fresh air for a little walk. We would go to this magical place called the sugar bush that had thousands of maple trees that would all be tapped in the spring. They were so old and glorious; I hugged one each day and gained courage from their solid strength. Over the next few weeks of March, I started to notice an improvement, but I knew something was still awry because I still had so much pain in my stomach. Finally, one day while I was in my whole-foods store verging on hopeless, I opened up about what was going on with my health to the store owner. I then asked her if she knew of a holistic practitioner in the area that maybe could help me? Please?

She pulled out two cards, and the first one she pushed my way said "Naturopath." This woman had been practicing in the area for a few years, she said. The second card said "Nelda, Holistic Health Educator" and she told me Nelda had been practicing for twenty-two years. So then I asked her whom she would pick for me, and she gently pushed Nelda's card all the way forward on the counter as if to say, "This is the lady you need," and she was so right.

The next week, I headed to Nelda's not knowing if I could even climb the stairs, but I slowly clambered up them and made it to her office. She started talking while muscle-testing me and I had no idea what was going on. Certainly no doctor had ever taken this much time to get to know me. I told her whom I had been to see and what they had said and she just kept on doing her work. I was so very tired. **NTS:** Being a young, vibrant woman in the prime of my life but dragging my ass around feeling like I haven't slept in three days is really hard. Remember that I believe my body has the potential to heal itself with the right nutrition and healing practitioners. Also, that there is healing help out there for me; I just need to *keep asking.*

Nelda then sat me down and said she was surprised that I had been able to drag my bag of bones in there, as she had never seen someone so low on magnesium. I was filled with warmth because finally I had found someone who understood how I was feeling and whom I could talk to about how to heal me. She also said that my body was utilizing so much magnesium that it couldn't catch up, so no wonder my intestines were a convoluted mess, leaving me bed-ridden with crippling cramps. Well, maybe she didn't say exactly that, but she did say that I needed magnesium, stat! So she sent me on my way with two tinctures and a huge bottle of magnesium. I swear, I started to notice the difference in days. I started walking upright again and even smiling. I had gotten my life back! I felt even better in the days to come, and I was so thankful to be able to walk and sneeze without pain. I knew I had a ways to go, but I was willing to do it on my own time and get back to my life, so I got online and re-booked my ticket to Dubai.

As I flew into Dubai for a third time in seven months, something felt different. All that focus on me and my body had given me a real appreciation for what I had. When I got back to my office, I found out that time had marched on without me and that my job was gone. I didn't worry, though, because I had this feeling that I was going to be okay. So while they looked for a new position for me, I took the time to reach out to new people.

I started going to Jumeirah Beach on weeknights to hear my new friend Zane sing on the balmy shores of the Gulf. To this day, it is one of my favorite memories. His beautiful voice would flow out on the waves and reach me in my soul. I would dance and sway. It was also as close as I wanted to get to a man at that point; anything else would have been too much. This was my time to just be with me, and all I was open to was friendship in groups with select men. When he wanted to hang out with just me, I suggested a group hangout instead.

Reflection: What will you do during your YOM when a guy wants to start an intimate relationship with you? There is no right or wrong answer; I will just say that the longer you take to focus on yourself in your YOM, the stronger your relationships will be in the future because you will have put your healing first. You are worth the wait.

Chapter 8

MYOM: April
Shake Yer Money Maker

A nyone who knows me will tell you that I *love* to dance! When I was unable to sneeze or walk properly, I couldn't dance either, and this was one of the things I was so desperately sad about losing. Dancing is deeply connected to a woman's sensuality, and not being able to dance while feeling the music run through my body was a great loss. Embodied dancing is also one of those things that they frown upon for women in UAE, and I even remember getting scolded once by my boss when she saw me moving to the music in my car! I was in my groove, and I thought I was in a private space, but I guess it wasn't. No matter where I am, though, I will never stop moving my body, no matter how much shame some other person tries to inflict on me. **NTS:** Car dancing is liberating, as is any kind of dancing that liberates my energy, which is important for my health.

Now that I'd had time away from Hamad to really take care of me and my body, I felt confident from being in such a healthy and, dare I say it, sexy soul vessel. Because of my new confidence in my body and spirit, I felt up to the challenge of a dance-a-thon put on for Westerners. Motown Mania came to Yaz Island in Abu Dhabi only 45 minutes away, so I dressed up and texted my guy friends Zane and Madesh to get down there and shake their money makers with me. **NTS:** Moving my body to music that I love has nothing to do with any man unless I want it to; in that space it was just about me and the joy I owned at being connected to my body. I need to share with my women friends that soul dancing is just pure unadulterated liberation.

When I got to the club, I began to shake my money maker right away. I have never had a problem being the lone dancer, because there is always somebody sitting down who admires my courage and will jump up to dance with me. Others started joining me one by one until the dance floor was full. By the end of the night, I was grooving my body on stage in pure glory with Madesh cheering me on. We were having so much fun, even if our other friend Zane couldn't make it out. When it came to audience participation and deciding on a winner of the contest, my joy at being able to move (finally!) enveloped the crowd and they cheered me on to win! I had *never* had this much fun with Hamad, because he never wanted to get to know me for who I really was. Madesh, on the other hand, cheered me on, and I felt like I had made a really good new friend. **NTS:** Just because I've taken a year off men does not mean they have taken a year off me. Prepare to be pursued.

Later that evening, Zane's wife called in a rage saying that I was sexting him with the "come and shake your money maker" text message. I had to reassure her that I certainly was not "sexting," and that I had no interest in another woman's man. Madesh also talked with Zane's wife to let her know that I was doing a YOM and that she had nothing to worry about. Hopefully this discussion with Madesh gave her pause. But I will say this: If a man lets, or shall I say encourages, me to be jealous of another woman, it shows a huge lack of character on his part. I hope I'd have enough faith in myself to leave a man who played mind games like that.

Precisely because Zane played games like this with his wife's head and heart, I felt that he was not going to be a good friend for me. I ended the friendship in a follow-up call later that night where I explained all of this. I don't know if before MYOM I would have had the courage to tell him everything I thought, but I did now. Honestly, it was a bit intimidating setting such stringent boundaries, but as I kept speaking my truth it became less and less limiting and more and more liberating. I hope my truthfulness on that call helped his wife and helped him be a better man. **NTS:** I am always too good to be someone's second best (aka mistress).

On the way home, I felt a real love blooming for Madesh, who was letting me be me, with no attempt at reeling me in and tamping me down. Still, I held back. After only four months of MYOM, I wasn't going to give in so easily. To be very honest, I felt I owed it to my future partner and to myself to stick to it, if we were to have any hopes of a successful relationship in the future. As the weeks passed and I felt more and more sure of my direction, I was really glad I had not brought Madesh into *my* world. I chose to lessen the lines of communication with him and focus on me, and we didn't see each other for a month.

Reflection: Do you often feel jealous when you're in a relationship? Why do you feel that is? This isn't about pointing fingers, but ask yourself, why would you want to be with someone you don't trust?
Fun Reflection: Wanna give soul dancing a try and see how good it makes you feel? Download your favorite song and get groovin'. I wanna see lips moving, shoulders shaking, and your head bobbing. Enjoy!

Chapter 9

MYOM: May–June
Spring Fever

When Madesh and I saw each other again a month later at a dance party, I felt joy and pain all wrapped up in one. I had missed his friendship and wanted to lean on him for support, but I knew that if I didn't stand on my own two feet right now I would slip back into my pattern of relying on a man to make me happy (even though it never ended up working). Daily, I had been going deep into me and my patterns of being with men whom I had nothing in common with except that they liked and approved of me. I now knew I needed to *love and approve* of me (thanks Louis).

Still, when Madesh saw me, we flew into each other's arms for a warm embrace, but because that's a no-no in the UAE, we quickly parted. We went inside the club to talk and to hide from the eyes of a country that can jail people for public displays of affection. Unfortunately, Madesh ruined our reunion by professing his unyielding love for me. I was so tender and so new at being me; it all felt like too much. So I had a drink, and then another, and started slipping into an old pattern as comfortable as broken-in heels. Then, of course, we left the club together, as per my well-worn pattern.

I know what you are thinking; I thought it too, because I felt overwhelmed with emotion and knew how much easier it would be to just do what I had always done. But no, we didn't hook up. He could have come up with me to my apartment, but instead I think he sensed that it would've been a bad idea to break the trust that we had in each other. We lingeringly kissed on the cheek goodbye and I went up to my apartment alone. Who knew this year was gonna be such a test?

As days and nights passed and life increasingly got better, I was able to grow my group of soul sisters, which was a must in MYOM. I would go to creative club meetings, raw-food potlucks, raw yoga, holistic days, and dance and dance. I kept up with my meditations and my mantras, as they actually helped improve many of my relationships. I was making my life amazingly rich, first on the inside, then out.

One day I found this little jazz bar down on The Palm and totally got struck in the heart by the drummer in the house band. We got to know each other over the next month, and he was so good-looking, kind, and funny, I didn't know if I'd to be able to stick to my resolution. I suppose you can look at it one of two ways: I totally fell off the wagon and hooked up with him, *or* I hooked up with him *only* once. The next day when we sat and chatted, he told me he had no intention of ever introducing me to his family. Here it was, my old pattern of rushing into intimacy without being clear about what I want. This was a great example of exactly why I needed a YOM. **NTS:** If I share my wants about what I need in a relationship with a partner *after* I hook up with him, it's usually too late to establish those boundaries. I need to not be afraid to speak up for myself from the get-go.

I declared to myself that my YOM was still in full effect, even if I had taken a little detour. At least I had learned a valuable lesson: slow down! Knowing a guy for a month is just scratching the surface of who he is, and sharing my body with him that quickly is too fast. Thank goodness it was time to go home for summer vacation and get away from all this drama. I was told that my brother had taken ill, but apparently it wasn't anything to worry about. At least that's what they said...

Reflection: If, or when, you fall off the wagon during your YOM, how will you get back on it? How will you keep your promise to yourself to really get to know your needs and wants?

Chapter 10

MYOM: July
A Man Who Taught Me to Put Myself First

What did a "year off men" mean to me? Was it just dating? Did it also apply to friends and family? I decided MYOM was specifically in the romance department and that perhaps I could grow from an experience with my brother who was very dear to me and who could teach me to take care of myself even if he needed a lot of care. I was blazing a new trail of what it meant for me, but it was a must to stay healthy while dealing with this new family crisis now that my brother was sick.

My mom (like so many other mothers out there) sets the exhausting precedent of continually depleting herself to be there for everyone else while ending up frazzled and, understandably, a little tender sometimes. Therefore, I decided to do the opposite and fill up my *inner well* first by eating really healthy food, doing yoga, and taking time out to meditate every day. I knew that if I did that I'd have enough "well water" to actually help with my family and not sacrifice my own health. **NTS:** Sacrifice and martyrdom only serve for a limited time, and then I wind up feeling depleted and resentful. It's much better for me to take a time out and replenish myself so I have extra to give to others. In the words of one of my beloved teachers, Thich Nhat Hanh, "The best way out is in."

I knew my brother hadn't been feeling well, but when I arrived home that summer, I was in for a shock. My brother had gotten so ill that I had to go straight from the airport to the hospital to see him. When I arrived, I found out that he had caught a rare brain infection. It was so rare that it was said there was a greater chance of being struck by lightning (which has actually happened in my family—twice). I saw him coding blue that day at the hospital. It was very painful for me to watch and even worse to feel. The doctors rushed in with the crash cart while my brother was turning blue, choking, gagging, and vomiting, and I was clearly hysterical. For a flash I thought, Fuck! Did I come home to see him die?! No, I told myself. No.

From all the work I had done in the past months, I knew I had the ability to paint the future positive with my thoughts, so right there in the hospital hallway, while the doctors were clearing his airway, I started to think him, see him, and feel him well. I began visualizing his wedding. It was the happiest event I could imagine he would be willing to hold on for. He wasn't even engaged yet, but in my visualization he was marrying his current girlfriend and I was eating wedding cake, dancing, giving a toast, the works. I could have even told you how the cake tasted.

The doctors stabilized my brother, who had been choking on his own vomit. I was angry and I went in at them on a rage. Not my finest moment, I'm sure, but I was livid. He had been sick for months and he was just getting worse; what were they doing for him except giving him awful drugs? What were they doing for his wellness, I asked, and they stared back at me blankly. Clearly, wellness was a different paradigm for them. Of course in this triage situation I was grateful for the doctors' help, but he needed more than just that. It looked as though his wellness and energetic healing was going to be up to me and my family from now on.

Every day, my whole family went to the hospital, and almost every day for more than a month I would get up, meditate, and drive an hour and a half to the hospital to spend all day with my brother, feeding him and energizing him to health. Along with everything everyone else was doing, I juiced him the best organic juices, green smoothied him the leafiest greens, whole food-ed, Reiki-ed, and mantra-ed him out. What the doctors thought of me, I don't know. However, one day the nurses pulled me aside and asked me a ton of questions about the delicious living food I was bringing my brother every day and how I had come to this type of healing. I told them it had been part of my own healing journey these past few months, and they acted thankful for the extra care I was bringing him. Of course, it was only because I had brought it to myself first that I was able to do it for him.

As far as taking time off men, at this point no exes were calling to see how I was coping. It was very clear that this time, I was really off men. During that very scary time for me and my family, I felt it was my duty to take a day off from the hospital here and there to keep myself healthy so that I had extra energy to then pour into my brother's food and healing. It would have been an easy time to fall into someone's arms, but so far I hadn't.

I didn't have a local spiritual community because before Dubai I had lived on the West Coast for almost a decade, so my sisterhood was 3,000 miles away when I really could have used their support. I had done more than enough work on my own for now, and I really wanted to fly out west and be with them. So when my brother got the green light from the hospital that he was ready to go home in mid-August, I saw my opportunity to go and be with the friends I had left a year earlier.

I was so thankful that my brother had recovered, but I hadn't realized the toll his sickness had taken on me as a caregiver. I denied for that whole time that anything wayward was going to come about due to his hospitalization, but in doing that I really denied parts of myself and my emotions that needed to be expressed. **NTS:** Denying my feelings builds up tension in my body and has the potential to make me act out. In the future, be honest about my feelings and feel where the tension gets stored in my body. Be present to the sensations and just breathe.

I realize now that because my brother had the courage to look death in the eye, he healed from that trauma. He healed with an acceptance that I am just learning about life and death. When death came knocking at his door, he made his peace with it, but I resisted it, even denied it. Now I see that admitting our inevitable passing one day brings in actual hope of rebirth right now. During MYOM, this important man in my life taught me the invaluable lesson of putting myself first, living in the present, accepting what is, and doing whatever you need to do to make the future what you want it to be.

Reflection: What's one way you sacrifice your spirit for others even when your body says no? What could you do differently to put yourself first, so that in return you have more to give to others?

Chapter 11

MYOM: August
Tuff City: You Ain't Kidding!

P erhaps it was a reaction to the intensity of the time I had spent with my brother at the hospital, but when I got out west to Tofino, also known as "Tuff City," to see my framily (friends + family), I may have acted out a little... I danced, surfed, and laughed up a storm. There will never be a more fun time than when you see all your dear friends in an awesome summer town with music and margaritas flowing. I was feeling good, my brother was well, I was super healthy, perhaps even glowing. I was having so much fun and I felt truly home. Then, two things happened. First: I said, Screw my year off men; I'm gonna have some fun! And second: My back went out. Bugger.

This is how it started: On a rare warm night in Tuff City, I danced and danced and went wild and free. This guy I had known socially for years, Toby, took notice of me, and we danced for the rest of the night. When the after-party went back to my girlfriend's house where I was staying, Toby would not let me out of his sight. He got me drinks, held my hand, and wrapped his arm around my shoulder.

This dynamic was all very familiar; there were many nights when after going out and having a few drinks and dancing, a good-lookin' fella and I would hook up. **Extra-Important NTS:** If a guy is lovin' me up on the dance floor and really digs me, he will wait until we are sober so we can get together again to actually get to know each other. If, on the other hand, he wants to hook up right then and there, in all likelihood he's just looking to get laid and it's going to be a very brief affair—and most likely not a very satisfying one.

Sexuality and spirituality had just never gone together for me before, but I was just learning to recognize this. I knew that if I believed in having a real connection with a guy, I needed to be sober and clear when being with him. I know I'm worth a sober guy wanting to get to know me. And if you, like me, have had to have a few drinks in the past to loosen up, perhaps it's ourselves we need to work on first, before being with any man.

Of course I didn't have that insight then, so after a night chillin' with the band and laughing with friends, Toby came back to the guest house with me and we started making out. My commitment to MYOM was waning again, and yet this time it definitely didn't feel so right. Toby was an okay kisser, but I could tell he was doing all this just to get something from me; he was only *giving* to *get*. But all I could think was, Holy hell, slow down! He then offered some serious sexy services that gave me pause, but something in my heart said a big NO. I gently pushed him away and said it would have to wait; I was taking it very slow. The fact that I did this with three margaritas coursing through my veins was a testament to how serious I was about an authentic connection. So Toby walked out the door and headed back home.

The next morning, I was revved-up, turned on and confused from our kissing session, and all of a sudden I regretted not gettin' some while the gettin' was good. However, it was thankfully too late to do anything about it, because I had to drive four hours to see my cousins that afternoon. **NTS:** In a sacred sexual connection, the outcome of being together is a feeling of fulfillment, not of *wanting* because you weren't fulfilled in the first place.

Reflection: What patterns do you have when hooking up with guys that are a result of not setting healthy boundaries?

Chapter 12

MYOM: Later in August
Back Attack

While visiting my extended family, I decided to change my flight so I could see how things might play out with Toby, and that's when *it* happened. Horrifically enough, my back went out just hours after I changed my flight. I was in agony. No chance for getting frisky now. I was so upset. My trip that I had just extended was ruined. Clearly, I still had a lot to learn (which is fine, since that was the whole point of my YOM). **NTS:** Changing my plans for a guy makes me seem too available, and I actually am too available if I bend to his whims instead of standing up for myself. I will no longer change my major plans for a man. It throws me off my center by putting him at the center of my universe. The best way to meet the man of my dreams is to follow my own.

Of course, now that I look back on it, I know my body was telling me to keep my promise to myself and not to change my plans for some guy who really had no intention of being there for me. Now, my body really wanted me to buckle down and spend time with it. **NTS:** My body is my biggest teacher and compass for what's good for me. It's really important to listen to my body to hear the messages it wants me to hear. Or else it will *make* me listen! After surfing, dancing, drinking, and kissing the days away back home in Tuff and not taking care of my body, it'd had enough! I get it, body, loud and clear.

At the time, though, I had to get through six more days of suffering, driving, chiropracting, and massaging to get me ready to fly back East to my brother, who was so far doing well. It was excruciating and humiliating. It was at that moment that I wanted someone to take care of me, but where was Toby, anyway?

Obviously, I needed to take care of myself, which I hadn't been doing, and really it had nothing to do with Toby. I had to heal physically, as well as spiritually, on my own. What had I been thinking? That his hooking up with me after one drunken night meant that he wanted something more with me or that he would be there for me? There was part of my old pattern again, going in way too fast and expecting a Hollywood outcome. It was time to refocus on me. The bright side, however, is that if I hadn't whacked out my back, I wouldn't have stuck to taking care of myself sexually and spiritually. I think that was the most important thing for me to recognize: my body was rescuing me from selling myself short again.

To this day, I am so thankful that I actually turned Toby down that night. I love that my body made me keep my promise when I went to the hormonal dark side, wanting some guy to mess around with for what, one night? Not exactly a very emotionally satisfying or deep experience. **NTS:** I am worth so much more than one night. We all are. And if I hear the word *fuck,* I think, Actually, nobody wants to be "fucked," let alone get "fucked over." How loving is that?! Being intimate with someone is the perfect time to speak up about what I want physically and spiritually, so as to dodge any man who is just trying to use me. When I speak my truth and the man I'm with acknowledges and tries to understand my needs, that's a great sign that he's got the depth I deserve.

Reflection: How have you compromised your self-worth in order to get a guy to stay interested in you? What can you do in the future to honor your sexual-spiritual path?

Chapter 13

MYOM: September
Relapse

I returned home from out west to spend some wonderful time with my family before going back to Dubai. Although my back was still pretty bent out of shape, I was in good spirits because my brother was apparently doing well. However, on my way to the airport after my brief visit, I started to get a really strange feeling in my stomach and called my mom. She said she couldn't talk because my brother wasn't feeling well and she needed to take him back to the hospital to see what was up. Oh no, I thought, not again! I told her I would cancel my flight, but she said I should go and not worry; she would keep me posted. Now that was a terrible flight!

A week later in Dubai, I got the dreaded email that my brother needed brain surgery. I was a nervous mess. I called everyone I could back home and no one was picking up their phones, of course, because the hospital makes you turn them off. Thankfully, my cousin Celeste was around to remind me that flying home thinking, Oh, I hope he doesn't die, was not going to be energetically helpful. When she suggested I sit tight and envision him healthy and happy, I did, but it was the hardest thing I have ever done.

By October, my brother's health was getting better again, but he was still weak. I let my office know I was seriously considering going back to Canada because I felt so overwhelmed with emotion. But in the end I stayed in Dubai instead of rushing home, because I recognized that he just needed time for his body to heal too.

Reflection: What trying situation are you now experiencing that would benefit from your envisioning the best outcome? Don't deny reality;

embrace it. Then, once you have felt the truth in your body, breath into it and let it dissipate. From there, transcend it by visualizing a positive outcome.

Chapter 14

MYOM: October
Yogilates

I remember walking into the yogilates studio in Dubai like it was yesterday. The red door told me this was not one of your run-of-the-mill stodgy workout joints, and I had a feeling that inspiration was waiting on the other side. As I walked in, I was greeted with the oranges, reds and blues of the tapestries that adorned the walls. I let the rich colors soak into me. Then, as I moved further in, I was joined by my new coach and soon-to-be-friend, Kara.

Kara and I went into the private coaching room and before I knew it, we were talking about my brother and all the stress I had been under. Going through all of it mostly on my own in a foreign country had been so hard, and tears sprang from my eyes as I told her everything. Since Hamad, my fall off the wagon, and my brother's illness, I needed a larger spiritual network and I recognized that it was time to grow it. Then I started talking to Kara about how I had been in a show before I left for the Middle East. When I had asked the director why she had chosen this particular play, she said it was because the play was a surefire way to meet kick-ass soul sisters. So, since I wanted a stellar community of soul sisters, a dream to direct and produce an all-woman show in Dubai started to unfold.

This studio was not only magical because of what bloomed in me there, but because the studio brought together so many people trying to connect. I took a few pamphlets from the bulletin board and started on my new spiritual journey in Dubai, a place where choosing spirituality over religion is a very foreign concept. The tide was certainly changing. In only ten months, so much had happened to make me change for the best. I wondered what wonderful people I would meet on my new journey.

Reflection: _In your YOM, you will need lots of support. What can you do right now to connect with some soul sisters who will encourage and support you on your journey? Perhaps you could team up with a friend to do your YOM together?_

Chapter 15

MYOM: November
Soul Sisters Everywhere

About the time I started making posters for the play I wanted
to produce and direct, the bulletin board at the studio was
filled with amazing things to do—at a price. There was also a
posting for free meditation classes at a beautiful local home, and
my interest was piqued. Gone were the days when my soul could
be satisfied by endless drinking and going out to bars. How could
you meet like-minded people when the music was too loud and
the smoke too thick to even see or hear each other? I think many
others were feeling that too, and there was quite a crowd for the
free meditation meet-up.

In the beginning of my free meditation classes, my teacher
was encouraging and kind. I was getting back on my feet after
my back being so terrible, and I felt that maybe this group was
the answer to my isolation. The best part of the free meditation
class was that I also found a Reiki practitioner in amongst the
meditation crowd. The wonderful thing about her was that she
held a free meet-up too, one where no one was trying to sell me
anything or make me believe what they believe. Lara, the Reiki
master, reminded me of my best friend from home, and I felt
very comfortable with all of the light practitioners I met through
her. No one there was better than anyone else, and no one had
power over any other. That wonderful group became my spiritual
community, which was something I so desperately needed.

Interestingly enough, Lara became one of my first coaching
clients and the most dear friend I could have ever made over there
or anywhere. I remember many a night talking over noodles and
laughing. She was and still is my true soul sister, a woman I can
talk to about anything and who never judges me. She was there

to support me with everything going on with my brother and MYOM and I wish every woman a soul sister like that. I will forever have gratitude to the universe for placing her in my life, and my heart will always be open to any pure soul such as hers. The great thing is that I am blessed with many soul sisters, and I know there are many more out there just waiting to be met.

Reflection: Think about the type of person you want in your life. Have you ever heard that you must be who you want to be with? It's so true! Now is the time to transform yourself into being the person you have always wanted in order to attract exactly that.

Chapter 16

MYOM: December

One Year Wrap-Up and What I Now Know

By December, I got a call from my brother that he had gotten the all-clear from his doctor and had just proposed to his girlfriend—he was well enough to get married (I mean I did help manifest it for him!). So much had happened in the last year—getting sick and being heartbroken, leaving my work, healing, returning to work, my brother falling ill and getting better, and my back breaking down. It had been a time of self-love and constant (although sometimes resistant) growth, but it made me stronger.

It was a miracle that such a tumultuous time turned into such a healing time, and not just for me. It brought about some amazing changes in my family as well, such as my mom and dad bonding again after a divorce years prior, and the internal shifts caused by my brother's illness leading him to choose to add to his life by finally proposing to his girlfriend of five years! For me, I was the most physically and spiritually healthy I had been in years, and I felt spectacular. It was a complete 180 from the painful Christmas a year prior, and I was so thankful.

When I returned to Dubai in the new year, I started putting up posters for auditions for the underground all-female show I'd been dreaming of putting on. I decided to present a little play that I felt would be helpful, perhaps even empowering. You may have heard of this play: it's called *The Vagina Monologues*, and this kick-ass little show was the one my director had said years ago would bring in many like-minded women, and the one that my Pilates instructor had been so jazzed about being part of. I already had her as a cast member, and I hadn't even held auditions yet! There was no better time for me to organize this transformative show because I wanted to meet even more soul sisters, grow my community, and be there for other women lost in this Middle Eastern sea of expats. The money raised would go to help end violence against women and girls, and I couldn't think of a more needed place to do it in. **NTS:** Was I crazy for putting on an illegal show that could maybe get me jailed, deported, or, worse, hurt? Why was it so forbidden to sexually empower women in the Middle East? I believed in this show. I felt that the women there were yearning for it, and if I didn't do it, who would?

I decided that since gaining strength from MYOM I was going to be strong for my soul sisters who needed my support. There were so many women I saw over there who were struggling to live their soul's purpose. I was going to try to give back to as many of these women as I could, women who had given so much to all the men in their lives, quite often thanklessly. They needed something for them, and I was going to bring it the best I could.

As MYOM (or *my om,* as I affectionately came to refer to it) came to a close, I could sense more seeds of growth and potential that needed watering in me. What would I do after MYOM? I had the play, but was there more I could do to grow? I felt for the first time that I'd really taken care of myself, and it felt amazing. My body and spirit were repaying me for such devotion to myself and I didn't plan on going back to the way I had been a year earlier. It had been a challenge, with more than a few bumps in the road, but I'd come out stronger and more put together than I'd ever been. What I knew for sure was that MYOM was invaluable to me. I had learned so much, and I couldn't imagine my newly abundant inner life without having done it.

<u>*Reflection:*</u> *What can you bring to your inner soul sister that will help you grow your sisterhood? It doesn't have to be illegal… that's just how I roll, when needed.*

Part III

Epilogue

It's been almost two years since I took MYOM, and so many things have changed for me on the inside that it's rippled out and turned my world upside down in a great way. For example, I left the Middle East, passing up a big financial opportunity to renew my job contract so I could start a business *I love* coaching and teaching women solo tantra techniques for everyday sensual-spiritual living—*sans man*! I'm also working on my second book, about how I kept living my truths to the best of my ability after all I had learned in MYOM.

As I continue to evolve, I am no longer "grateful" if just any man likes me; I know I am totally enough (and so are you). Not perfect, but perfect for the right partner. Certainly, to come to that conclusion took me stepping out of the dating game to set up my own playing board where I never lose, only learn. I'm not saying I don't get knocked back a peg or two by slipping into old relationship patterns here and there, but at least I recognize what's happening and can do something about it now!

MYOM helped me learn so much about what I want that even if I have setbacks I can keep moving forward now. This is uber-important, because when I didn't know what type of man I wanted to invite into my life or what type of relationship I wanted, I got everything from player to poser, and none of them were good for me. Now, in approaching relationships with men, I actually ask them what they want, to see if it's in alignment with what I want. Why bang my head against a brick wall if the man doesn't want the same things I do? No! Moving on! If he doesn't want a relationship, that's okay, but if I do want one, he is not the man for me, and I really need to look elsewhere instead of trying to change his mind (cuz does that ever really work?). Now I take my energy and focus on being the best version of me, so that when I'm ready for partnership, I attract someone who is the best version of themselves too.

It was so worthwhile taking MYOM, because it grew me in ways I didn't know I could grow. It made me grow within and root down really deep into my soul. I would do it again, too, if I ever noticed myself being knocked off my center, but so far I've been able to take daily care of myself with meditation and tantra so that doesn't happen. Amen! If you have never tried a YOM, I highly recommend it to give you clarity, space, and connection with yourself that you can only get from growing within.

This book is my sincere gift to you, my soul sister. I hope this book will support you (or a friend) when you decide to take a year off, or even a month off, the "search" for a man, so you can search within. When you do, you will be amazed at what you find, and probably never look back!

Final Reflection: Do you think you need to take a YOM? If so, are you ready to make the commitment to yourself today? Enjoy your year off and find extra support on my web page any time at kellyalexander. org. Good luck to you, my sweet soul sister.

About the Author

KELLY ALEXANDER is a Certified Transformational Coach. She specializes in relationship coaching for women teaching them Passion and Pleasure techniques through Tantra. She has a B.A. in psychology, fine art, and education from Western and Trent University. She is also a ten year Reiki practitioner. Regularly she spends her days laughing, dancing, running workshops and privately coaching women on the joy of integrating their spiritual and sensual lives. Kelly began her spiritual quest at the age of twelve when her grade school teacher taught her how to meditate. Twenty-two years later, she continues on her spiritual journey. She now lives in Canada, after an epic fifteen years of globe-trotting and growing. Kelly also has a monthly video blog with free relationship tips for women at www.kellyalexander.org. She wishes you well on your journey, whatever wonderful places it may take you.

CPSIA information can be obtained at www.ICGtesting.com
Printed in the USA
BVOW08s1954301213

340526BV00001B/3/P